Michael Jordan

Legendary Guard

by
Thomas S. Owens

The Rosen Publishing Group's
PowerKids Press™
New York

Published in 1997 by The Rosen Publishing Group, Inc.
29 East 21st Street, New York, NY 10010

First Edition

Book Design: Kim Sonsky

Photo Credits: Cover © Richard Kane/SportsChrome—USA; pp. 7 (both), 8, 15, 16, 18, 19, 20 (all) © AP/Wide World Photos; pp. 4, 9, 11, 19 © Archive Photos.

Owens, Tom, 1960–
   Michael Jordan : legendary guard / Thomas S. Owens.
      p.   cm. — (Sports Greats)
   Includes index.
   Summary: Profiles the basketball superstar, who retired from the Chicago Bulls at age thirty, played minor league baseball, and then returned to professional basketball in 1994.
   ISBN 0-8239-5090-5
   1. Jordan, Michael, 1963– —Juvenile literature. 2. Basketball players—United States—Biography—Juvenile literature. 3. Chicago Bulls (Basketball team)—Juvenile literature. [1. Jordan, Michael, 1963–
2. Basketball players. 3. Afro-Americans—Biography.] I. Title. II. Series: Sports greats (New York, NY)
GV884.J67095 1997
796.323'092—dc21   97-3864
                                                                           CIP
                                                                             AC

Manufactured in the United States of America

Contents

A Star Is Born

Michael Jeffrey Jordan was born on February 17, 1963, in Brooklyn, New York. He and his family soon moved to Wilmington, North Carolina. Michael's dad built a basketball court in the backyard on the grass so his kids could play together.

Michael enjoyed playing different kinds of sports. When he was in ninth grade, he played for his school's baseball, football, and basketball teams. In tenth grade, Michael tried out for the **varsity** (VAR-sih-tee) basketball team, but he wasn't chosen. At five feet, eleven inches, Michael wasn't tall enough—at least not according to the coach!

◀ Michael liked playing different kinds of sports. But he liked basketball the best. Maybe his dad, shown here with Michael, knew that when he built a basketball court in their backyard.

5
NBA

Things Are Looking Up

Michael was determined to make the varsity basketball team. He practiced his game all year. He also grew four inches. By eleventh grade, he made the varsity team. He played very well. As a senior, he averaged nearly 29 points a game. He was so good that he earned a basketball **scholarship** (SKOL-ur-ship) to go to the University of North Carolina. There he studied geography.

Because it was Michael's first year on the team, some people were surprised that he started every game. But Michael's jump shot won the national championship game that year for his team, the Tar Heels. People wondered how any nineteen-year-old newcomer could be so good.

Michael surprised everyone at the University of North Carolina by how well he played. ▶

Hello, NBA

In 1984, Michael finished his third year as a college basketball star. He was chosen to play on the U.S. Olympic basketball team. He helped the United States win a gold medal. Michael chose to leave school to try to play **professional** (pro-FESH-en-ul) basketball. During the National Basketball Association, or NBA, **draft** (DRAFT), Michael was ignored by the first two teams to choose players, the Houston Rockets and the Portland Trailblazers. They chose taller players. Choosing third, the Chicago Bulls found their future superstar. But Michael knew that his education was important. So he finished college over the next two summers.

◄ The Chicago Bulls had no idea how good Michael would turn out to be.

9

Making the Bulls Better

The year before Michael joined the Bulls, the team won 27 games and lost 55. During Michael's first two years on the team, the Bulls didn't do much better. They still had more losses than wins. But they made the play-offs both years. In 1986, Michael set a play-off record with a 63-point game against the Boston Celtics. The Bulls paid Michael six million dollars over the next seven years. That was the most money anyone had ever been paid to play for the NBA. Michael was becoming the NBA's best player. So why weren't the Bulls becoming the NBA's best team?

10

NBA

The Bulls had Michael, the NBA's best player, on their team. But they needed something ▶ else to become the NBA's best team.

On Top Three Times

Coach Phil Jackson

In 1990, the Bulls hired a new coach, Phil Jackson. That season, Coach Jackson helped the Bulls win their first championship ever. They had been trying for 25 years. Coach Jackson got the Bulls to try a new game plan. He wanted Michael and the rest of the team to share the **responsibility** (ree-spon-sih-BIL-ih-tee) of scoring.

With teamwork, the Bulls stayed champions for two more seasons. Michael won several NBA season scoring **honors** (ON-erz), as well as several Most **Valuable** (VAL-yoo-bul) Player, or MVP, awards. At the age of 30, after nine years with the Bulls, Michael wondered if there were any **challenges** (CHAL-en-jez) left for him in basketball.

◀ Under Coach Phil Jackson, Michael and the Bulls went on to win three NBA championships in a row.

13

Hello, Baseball

On October 6, 1993, Michael **retired** (ree-TYRD) from basketball. Michael wanted to try another sport—baseball. As a Little League star, Michael had dreamed of playing in the **major leagues** (MAY-jer LEEGZ). Michael joined the **minor leagues** (MY-ner LEEGZ) in 1994. He hoped to become an outfielder for the Chicago White Sox. But baseball was hard. In the minors, he batted only .202, and had more strikeouts than hits. Then, in 1995, no major league teams started the season because of a long **strike** (STRYK). Although Michael had said that he would never play basketball again, he decided to leave baseball and play for the Bulls again. He played the last seventeen games of the 1995 basketball season.

14

Michael played baseball for nearly two seasons. ▶

Back to Basketball

The Bulls were happy to have Michael back. Michael's new jersey number was 45. He had played so well that the Bulls retired his old jersey number, 23, when Michael retired. No other member of the Bulls could ever wear that number. Michael chose 45 because his older brother, Larry, had worn that number when he played basketball in high school.

With Michael back, the Bulls set a new single-season record with 72 wins and 10 losses. For the eighth season, Michael led the NBA in scoring. The Bulls beat the Seattle Supersonics in the final round of the play-offs. This was the fourth time that the Bulls had won the championship. Michael was named MVP for both the regular season and the championship games.

◀ "Never say never," was what Michael said to those who questioned his return to basketball.

Mike Likes ...

Off the court, Michael has many favorite things besides basketball. Steak and eggs is his favorite meal before a game. For every game, Michael wears a new and different pair of sneakers made by Nike. Each pair of sneakers is made from a mold of his foot for a perfect fit. At home, Michael likes baseball, bowling, and golf. He even built a putting green in the basement of his house. He likes to shoot pool, too. Most of all, he likes to spend time with his wife, Juanita, his sons, Jeffrey and Marcus, and his daughter, Jasmine.

Michael likes to do many things besides play basketball. He likes to play golf and spend time with his family. ▶

A Famous Face

Michael is so popular that many companies hire him to sell their **products** (PRAH-dukts). He is in many television commercials. His huge smile, dancing eyes, and shaved head are as famous as his flying slam-dunks. When Michael drank Gatorade, the commercial sang, "Be Like Mike." Michael has been on many Wheaties cereal boxes. Michael Jordan's, The Restaurant, is a famous place to eat in Chicago. Nike has made more than a dozen kinds of shoes named after "Air" Jordan. Michael played himself in the movie *Space Jam*, in which he played basketball with cartoon characters such as Bugs Bunny.

◀ Michael's smiling face helps sell many things, from sneakers to cereal.

21

Life After Basketball

   Michael has said that he won't play basketball forever. After the Bulls won their fourth championship in 1996, Michael said he would play for no more than two more years. The Bulls paid him $30 million to play for the 1996–97 season. This was a new record.

   Michael was one of the top players in the NBA. He had been on the best team many times. And he had set many NBA records. What challenge would Michael take on next? Would he become a professional golfer someday? Would he become a movie star? No matter where Michael goes, fans are sure he will always be a winner.

22

Glossary

challenge (CHAL-enj) Something that takes a strong interest and effort to do or finish.

draft (DRAFT) A time during which professional teams take turns choosing new players from college, high school, and other countries.

honor (ON-er) Credit for doing something very well.

major league (MAY-jer LEEG) Top-level professional baseball teams.

minor league (MY-ner LEEG) Lower-level professional baseball teams.

product (PRAH-dukt) Something that someone sells.

professional (pro-FESH-en-ul) To be paid for doing something.

responsibility (ree-spon-sih-BIL-ih-tee) Something that a person must take care of or complete.

retire (ree-TYR) To stop playing or working.

scholarship (SKOL-ur-ship) Money set aside to pay for a student-athlete's education once he or she has agreed to play for that school's team.

strike (STRYK) When players stop playing a sport in order to be better treated.

valuable (VAL-yoo-bul) Someone or something that is worth a lot to someone.

varsity (VAR-sih-tee) The highest team in a school sport.

23

Index